COB and THATCH

COB and THATCH

PAMELA EGELAND

DEVON BOOKS

First published in Great Britain in 1988 by Devon Books
Copyright © Devon County Council, 1988
ISBN 0 86114–816–9

British Library Cataloguing-in-Publication Data

Egeland, Pamela
  Cob and thatch
  1. South-west England. Thatched buildings. Architectural features.
  I. Title
  721′.5

Printed and bound in Great Britain by A. Wheaton & Co. Ltd

Produced by the Amenities and Countryside Officer, Peter Hunt, for the Amenities and Countryside Committee through the Property Department Director, Andrew Smy.

DEVON BOOKS
Official Publisher to Devon County Council

An imprint of Wheaton Publishers Ltd, a Pergamon Press plc company

Wheaton Publishers Ltd
Hennock Road, Marsh Barton, Exeter, Devon EX2 8RP
Tel: 0392 74121; Telex 42794 (WHEATN G)

SALES
Direct sales enquiries to Devon Books at the address above.

Trade sales to:
Town & Country Books, P.O. Box 31, Newton Abbot, Devon TQ12 5AQ.
Tel: 08047 2690

CONTENTS

ACKNOWLEDGEMENTS

The author wishes to thank David Lake and David Turbitt, Members of the Devon and Cornwall Master Thatchers Association, for their assistance with information on thatching.

Photographs are reproduced by permission of the following:

Peter Beacham (Conservation Section, Amenities & Countryside Division, Devon County Council Property Department): p. 70

The Beaford Archive, The Beaford Centre, Beaford, near Winkleigh, N. Devon (Tel: 08053 201): pp. 30, 40, 56 (upper), 66

Deborah Griffiths (Archaeologist, Dartmoor National Park Authority): p. 63

Graham Ward (Devon County Council Photographic Unit and Support Services, Property Department): pp. 11, 21, 74 (lower), 75, 88

Westcountry Studies Library: p. 25 (lower)

Photographs on p. 20 are from the Transactions of the Devonshire Association.

All other photographs are by the author.

Cover: Cottages at South Milton, Devon (J. C. Ticehurst)

Illustrations by Tony Whieldon.

1

HISTORY OF COB

Few domestic buildings relate to their surroundings as well as those constructed before the eighteenth century. Throughout the country, vernacular farmhouses and cottages owe their particularly sympathetic relationship with the landscape to the time in which they were built – a time when settlements and farmsteads were quite isolated, journeys difficult and generally limited to short distances and transportation of goods confined to those places which could be reached by sea or river. These factors enforced localized styles of building which gained their varied characteristics from the material used for their construction, and this was by necessity whatever was available close at hand.

Until specific social and economic developments started to become generally effective, the geology of each region was the fundamental influence on the material which could be used for local building purposes. In the region formed by the south-west peninsula this tended to remain the governing factor until somewhat later than other more accessible parts of the country. This was chiefly due to the difficulty of inter-communication, caused by the topographical features which not only divided Devon from its neighbouring counties to the east, but similarly cut off the upland areas of the county, leading to an insular way of life for the inhabitants. The ports of the South West were an exception to the isolation which lingered inland. By the late sixteenth century, an export trade was flourishing and the buildings of the port towns were among the first in the country to be influenced by architectural styles from the Continent, but it took nearly a century before new methods and ideas penetrated the upland areas. Meanwhile, most rural dwellings continued to be constructed in a simple and basic style with any form of decoration or variation in traditional detailing being dependent upon the wealth of the owner and locally available skills. The material with which these early Devon houses were built was that which was obtainable on or near the site – either stone or the earth itself, known as cob.

Cob and thatch villages: Dunsford, Inner Hope and East Budleigh. Many of the cottages shown here, and throughout this book, are Listed Buildings of Special Architectural or Historic Interest, classified as Grades I, II* or II. Buildings of exceptional interest (less than 5 per cent of Listed Buildings) are classified Grade I, those of special interest are Grade II, while some in this classification considered to be particularly important are Grade II*.

The geology of Devon consists basically of sandstones, shales and clays. These strata are dominated by the large granite mass of Dartmoor and there are other smaller areas of igneous rock in the south of the county. So in many regions a rocky sub-stratum readily provided ample stone for local building needs; these areas can be identified by the appearance of the cottages and farmhouses constructed from the various types. Chalkstone, flint, chert and New Red Sandstone can all be found in east Devon, pink and grey Devonian limestone appears in the South Hams, while in north Devon and on Exmoor, Old Red Sandstone is typical. Even the granite of Dartmoor yielded sufficient building stone from the naturally weathered-out blocks found in the clitters of rocky outcrops, before the development of the quarrying industry in the early nineteenth century.

However, those areas having a supply of stone were in the minority. Clay, shale and sandstones of the Carboniferous period make up the greater part of Devon's geological structure. Known as the Culm Measures, the bulk of these sub-strata extend south and east from the north-west coast to the southern edge of Exmoor, across the centre of the county to meet the granite boss of Dartmoor and then spreading over the border into Cornwall. Smaller pockets of similarly composed strata also occur elsewhere and all these areas were equally poor in the provision of stone suitable for constructional purposes. It is in these regions that Devon's wealth of cob buildings is to be found.

The use of unbaked earth for building is not, of course, peculiar to Devon; on the contrary, its use has been universal from time immemorial for all types of structure, from primitive mud huts to fashionable houses of comparatively recent date, but there were many differences in the ways in which it was utilized. In this country alone, variations of cob are to be found in many regions. The differences result from the basic composition of the soil; this determines the additives needed to cause the unbaked earth to set, the manner in which the material is built up, the thickness of the walls and, not least, the name by which it is known. Thus, to quote a few examples, in East Anglia the wet earth was mixed with straw, then shaped into rectangular blocks which were allowed to dry naturally before being used. This is called clay lump and it is very similar to the adobe of Spain. Wichert consisted of a chalky-based mud, which again was mixed with straw and is local to only a small area of Buckinghamshire. Pisé was another version of rather different character: it was a much drier mix altogether of earth and gravel, and shuttering was used for its construction. Introduced into France by the Romans, pisé is a traditional building material in many countries.

These and other systems of building with unbaked earth were as common in former times as is the use of brick today, but cob itself is known in very few areas outside Devon. Although none of the very earliest cob buildings still

Cob farmhouse with thatched and slate roof. The original open hall house (right) dates from the late fifteenth century and the remainder was added during the seventeenth century. Listed Grade II*. Hill, Christow.

This cottage typifies the simple character of a late-seventeenth/early-eighteenth-century cob and thatch building. The slate lean-to roof is a later addition. Dartington.

exists, there is evidence that this material was used here from the thirteenth century, continuing until well into the nineteenth century for the more humble cottages. Many of the cob houses and cottages standing today originate from the sixteenth and seventeenth centuries and they are by no means confined to simple labourers' dwellings, but include very substantial and important houses such as Raleigh's birthplace, Hayes Barton near East Budleigh. These survivals contribute to the great number of buildings of unbaked earth which still remain in Devon, more than in any other county. The reason for this large number is uncertain. It may be due to the material having been used over a wider area and for a greater time span than elsewhere, or it may simply mean that the advice of the old Devon saying 'all cob wants is a good hat and a good pair of shoes' has been taken seriously and has prevented penetration of damp to the top and base of the walls, where cob is most vulnerable.

As the influences which had started in the major ports of the county spread further afield, the use of cob began its gradual decline. In its place came earth in baked form, which in the beginning was probably an inadvertent by-product of

Hayes Barton, East Budleigh:
sixteenth-century manor house,
modernized in the late nineteenth
century, Hayes Barton was leased
to Walter Raleigh senior in 1551 by
the owner, John Duke. Listed
Grade II*.

the export trade in wool from Devon to the Continent. The first bricks to be seen here since Roman times were carried primarily as ballast on the outward voyages of Dutch trading ships, and, in the first instance, these may have been used for building for purely economic reasons. However, the popularity of brick grew when it was realized that these small blocks of baked earth provided a much quicker and more convenient method of construction than the laborious processes which were involved in cob building. In the Culm Measures, brick became a fashionable alternative to cob for wealthy landowners, who could afford to rebuild or extend their houses with bricks, probably manufactured on the site. For most of the inhabitants of these regions, however, cob remained the cheapest and most practical building material until the advent of the Industrial Revolution.

During the early nineteenth century, technological developments effectively brought to an end some 600 years of building tradition in Devon. The quarrying industry provided stone and slate, brickyards produced both bricks and clay

Cob and thatch, Art Nouveau style: designed by Ernest Gimson in 1910, the cob was 'made of stiff sand found on the site; this was mixed with water and a great quantity of long wheat straw trodden into it'. Eight men took three months to build the 3ft thick walls to eaves height, the thickness being later pared down to 2ft 6in. Listed Grade II*. Coxen, East Budleigh.

tiles, and the inauguration of the railway system made transport of these materials easier. The character of towns and villages began to change as these alternative materials were used for new buildings, replacing the cob and thatch of preceding years.

However, although the tradition of cob building lay dormant for a time, it was not completely forgotten. There was a resurgence of interest during the early part of the twentieth century, when a group of eminent architects of the Art Nouveau period rejected the new technology of the Victorians and adopted a style of building which laid emphasis on the use of natural materials and traditional craftsmanship. Walls of unbaked earth featured in many of the houses designed by the members of the Arts and Crafts movement, but they showed little of the traditional character of cob cottages; this was a style of architecture which exaggerated the effect of natural materials and their characteristics. One of the architects involved with the movement at this time, Clough Williams-Ellis, of Portmeirion village fame, subsequently developed an interest in the practicalities of all forms of unbaked earth construction, advocating a return to these systems when a shortage of almost all other building materials followed the First World War. He failed to raise much enthusiasm and cob has remained a building material of the past, except for the recent construction of some minor structures promoted by the current revival of interest in earlier crafts.

As time is of prime importance in everything nowadays, it seems unlikely that cob, or any of its related systems, will be considered to be a realistic proposition in the future. It is, therefore, all the more important that Devon's cob houses are properly conserved.

2

BUILDING WITH COB

The basic ingredient of all the systems of building with unbaked earth – cob, clay lump, pisé and wichert – is mud; but mud on its own is not a stable enough material for building purposes. If it is not reinforced, it will crack and fall apart as soon as it is completely dry, and conversely, if it becomes wet again it will quickly return to mud.

To make earth strong enough to stand in vertical form it needs the addition of a binding material containing lime. In the heyday of mud buildings, this additive could have been gravel, chalk, sand or shilf, all of which substances could be present in the soil, depending upon the locality; in the event that the earth contained no lime at all, straw made an efficient substitute. Some of the different methods of mud building have already been described and like the clay lump of East Anglia, the earth of the Culm Measures was lacking in lime and was mixed with straw, but the similarity between the two ends there. The early technology which was applied to building with clay lump and pisé was not used in the construction of cob, probably because there was little timber to spare for shuttering or moulds in the cob-building areas. This difference in method had a distinct effect on the characteristics of the buildings: whereas walls of clay lump and pisé were fairly straight and regular, those of cob had an informal and uneven appearance, owing to their having been built up without the benefit of any guide lines but entirely by the eye of the builders, some truer than others.

The whole process of construction with cob was a very laborious and time-consuming task, usually carried out by a semi-skilled team of four men. The techniques employed were often those which had been handed down from generation to generation and more often than not the team was a family concern which was responsible for all building operations in the locality, possibly managing to complete one cottage in a year. The slow rate of progress was due to the necessity of allowing each layer of cob to dry out thoroughly before proceeding with the next layer – the golden rule of building with mud.

The informality of cob appears as an extension of the landscape. Dartington and Dunsford. (Note: the date depicted probably relates to an earlier building on the site.)

This process was of course unaided by any mechanical means but relied solely on climatic conditions, so while the usual aim was to start work in the spring and finish before the beginning of winter, the completion of a house could take as long as two years under extreme circumstances.

The only exception to the observance of the drying-out rule was on occasions when the objective was not to build an enduring home, but simply to establish ownership of a plot of land. Family and friends were roped in to help the prospective owner complete the building of his cottage in a single day. This was no more than a simple one-roomed shelter, but provided that work was commenced at dawn and finished by dusk, complete with roof covering it and a fire burning in the hearth, this was sufficient to establish ownership of the land on which the cottage stood. Despite being put up in such a hurry and without any of the proper precautions against the cob becoming damp, surprisingly some of these early structures are said to have stood for as long as 150 or 200 years. In any event, even if they collapsed after a short time, the owner had gained a free site and could always rebuild at his leisure, so all was not lost.

The cob houses and cottages which still stand today were built with much more care and a proper observance of all the requirements. The first thing to be provided was the 'good pair of shoes', or the plinth. This was normally built in stone, since small quantities of stone could generally be found on or near the building site, even in the areas of clay and shale sub-strata. In some regions the plinth may have been built of brick, though this seems to have been uncommon in Devon, where the early use of brick was chiefly confined to chimneys. The stone used for the plinth could be rubble, chert, flint or shale, and this was built up to a height of 1 or 2 ft (30–60 cm) above the level of the ground and subsequently tarred. This coating not only gave added protections against rising damp, but also discouraged vermin from burrowing their way through the plinth. In the crudely constructed shelters mentioned above, where the cob was built directly off the ground, mice and rats could in this manner cause the eventual collapse of a wall.

The preparation of the cob took place as close as possible to the site selected for the house or cottage. The removal of the earth after mixing operations naturally left a hollow in the ground and this sunken area often became either the site for the privy or, in the case of a larger building such as a farmhouse, the site of the duckpond.

An area of approximately 20 sq.ft (1.8 sq.m) of earth was worked on at one time. Two of the building team would dig and turn the dry earth, the third would add the water as they worked and as this mixture gradually turned to mud, the remaining member of the team would supply pieces of chopped barley straw to be shovelled into the mix, which was of a fairly stiff consistency. This mixture was then well trodden to compact it together, either by the builders

themselves or by the less strenuous method of allowing farm animals to walk on it. The most experienced teams of men knew at a glance when the cob had been trodden sufficiently to achieve the correct consistency and when the first batch was ready the construction of the wall commenced. The team worked in pairs, two standing on the plinth, with the other two forking the wet mixture up to them to be spread along the top of the stone and compacted by treading again. Both the stone plinth and the base of the cob walling were very thick – between 2 ft and 4 ft (0.6 m and 1.2 m) – but each of the layers of cob which made up the full height of the wall was comparatively shallow, often less than 12 in. (300 mm).

In north Devon, the stone plinth was often the full height of the ground floor: elsewhere, it was usually 1–2ft above the ground, with a tarred finish, as can be seen in the two previous illustrations.

Constructing cob walls in north Devon early this century: traditional team of four laying cob and paring off the surplus.

As each layer was completed and well compacted, any surplus cob was roughly pared off from the faces of the wall and the top surface was covered with straw and left to dry. Here the presence of the straw probably served a dual purpose – providing protection against rain, as well as forming a key to bond in with the next layer of cob. At this point in the process, unless the weather was dry and hot and the cob likely to dry out while the next batch was being prepared, the building team might move to another site nearby. There they would prepare and spread a layer of cob for a second cottage and then, leaving that to dry, return to the first site, repeating the procedure until the walls had reached their intended height.

Until the end of the seventeenth century or thereabouts, cruck frames were quite often used in conjunction with cob construction, in both the simpler and grander types of dwelling. These timbers formed the main rafters for the roof and whereas in most parts of the country it is more usual to come across true crucks of curved timbers, in Devon these are commonly found to be in jointed form. The regional shortage of building timber may have been responsible for the use of jointed crucks, but the shorter straighter timbers did have a certain advantage in terms of causing less obstruction within the house. In a simple cottage the original crucks probably had a rather primitive appearance, but in larger houses they may be found to be quite sophisticated in details of carpentry and decoration.

The small domestic buildings of the sixteenth and seventeenth centuries were not usually built to any predetermined design and of course it was not necessary in those days to build to any specific standards related to heights of

Interior view of a cruck-framed cob house. Hill, Christow.

rooms or window sizes. These details were based on people's practical needs and experienced builders knew by eye alone the area and height necessary to meet these needs. Rooms were quite low and windows were small, just sufficient to allow the minimum amount of light to the interior, and there was usually only one window in each room. Window and door openings were not formed during the construction of the walls but were cut out of the hardened cob afterwards, ready for the carpenter – or, failing that, the local wheelwright – to make and fix timber frames. The small windows preserved the warmth provided by the thickness of the cob walls in winter, which were equally efficient in keeping the house cool in summer. The walls were completed on the outside with a protective covering of plaster or limewash, or occasionally both. The most commonly used colour finishes were cream, buff or pink – white appearing only infrequently.

The 'hat' which covered houses and cottages of cob was, almost without exception, thatch. It was also used to roof stone buildings before slate became available. Like cob, thatch has good insulating properties and with its steep pitch and generous overhang, it provided the walls below with protection from wet, throwing rain-water well clear of the building. Cob and thatch are materials which complement each other perfectly, neither having any hardness of line, both having an informal and rounded appearance. The current trend of replacing thatch with modern roofing materials such as asbestos slate is not recommended as the mechanical lines of the roof always provide an unhappy contrast with the irregularities of the walls below.

Perhaps one of the most easily recognizable characteristics of early cob buildings, apart from their curving and unevenly surfaced walls, are the rounded corners at each change of direction and to any projection. These occur because without the use of shuttering it was not possible to form a sharp angle by hand, so at these points the cob became thicker and was smoothed off into a curve. Since plumb lines were not used, walls often tend to lean inwards towards the roof and they are frequently found to be less thick at the top. There are two theories about the reason for this, neither appearing to prove any specific purpose. One explanation is that as the walls became higher the more difficult it was to maintain the full width of the base, whereas an alternative reason may be that a natural settlement of the cob occurred as more weight was added. Sometimes too the whole house followed the slope of the ground, the builder's eye being unable to judge correctly an imaginary water level.

Thatched houses and cottages built of cob are seen all over Devon, their exteriors still looking very much the same as they did when newly constructed, even though inside they probably contain modern conveniences. This is a result of much attention being given in recent years to the preservation of the

Rounded corners and projections characteristic of early cob buildings. Drewsteignton and Clyst St Mary.

The cob walls of this small cottage lean inwards towards the eaves: probably once a detached structure, it is now connected by a single-storey link to another property. Exeter.

character of regional buildings, which are all part of Britain's heritage. But some types of cob structures have not survived so well. One group in particular which has declined in numbers comprises farm buildings, including barns and outbuildings. This is probably a result of the technological changes which have occurred in farming techniques. Once so essential to farming operations, these small structures no longer seem suited to current practices and many of them, their roofs collapsed, have been left to decay as their cob walls gradually deteriorate from damp penetration.

Disused barns in north Devon: that on the right has been recently demolished but the other may be saved and converted.

Neglect of farm buildings is apparently quite traditional, as this early-nineteenth-century engraving by Samuel Prout seems to indicate!

Luckily, garden walls of cob have not suffered the same fate to any great extent. These were very popular during the eighteenth century as they provided warm and sheltered conditions which were excellent for growing fruit and they were built with just as much care as the walls to any dwelling. Complete with stone plinths and thatched or tiled cappings, they provide attractive features, winding alongside village streets. Their plinths were usually tarred to give protection to the base which was vulnerable to damage by a build up of soil in the garden, but above the plinth the cob was not always colour washed or plastered, so the natural colour of the earth of the region was exposed in tones of dark red, ochre or brown.

Garden walls of cob: thatched capping in East Budleigh and tiled capping in Dunsford; both walls are Listed Grade II in their own right.

3

HISTORY OF THATCH

The origins of thatch are just as ancient as those of cob, but unlike cob, thatch has a limited life and none that can be seen on a roof today is much more than half a century old. Depending upon the variety of thatch used and the climatic conditions of the area, it will usually be necessary to rethatch at any time between ten and sixty years.

The name 'thatch' comes from the old English version of the German word 'dach', meaning 'roof'. The original form of the word was 'thack' and this referred to virtually any material which could be used to provide cover to a dwelling. These materials all had one thing in common – they were always taken from locally available wild vegetation. Amongst those varieties known to have been used were turf, heather, bracken, brushwood and broom. These were abandoned later when marsh reeds came into use and the advent of cultivated crops brought the alternative of straw from wheat, rye and barley; of the latter, long straw from wheat is still used by thatchers today, as well as combed wheat reed and water reed.

From the end of the Roman occupancy of Britain to the twelfth century, thatch was the most commonly used roof covering throughout the country, with wooden shingles an alternative in areas where timber was plentiful. Needless to say, the fire risk was considerable in towns where the houses were both built of timber and roofed with thatch and, because of this risk, thatch was prohibited in London from the early thirteenth century for roofs to new buildings. Other major towns gradually followed suit, but in the cob regions of Devon such a decree was not practical as any other material was not only difficult to obtain, but would also have been considered too heavy to be supported by walls of unbaked earth. Despite its thickness, a cob wall is not very strong and too much loading on the top of it will cause it to bulge outwards; it will then be necessary to support it with buttresses to prevent it from falling down altogether. Although layers of thatch form quite a deep roof

The front wall of this farmhouse has been supported with four buttresses. Near Tipton St John.

covering, it is not as heavy as might be supposed and for support it needs only a lightweight framework nailed to the cruck frame or rafters, so the whole of the roof structure is both economical and practically suited to a building of cob.

Today thatched buildings are no more likely to be damaged or destroyed by fire than any other. The situation was very different in Medieval settlements. Most buildings then did not have chimneys: the hearth was in the centre of the room and the smoke escaped through a hole in the roof, thus increasing the risk of fire. Moreover, there were at that time no specific precautions or fire-fighting facilities and the villagers had to deal with smouldering thatch as best they could. Speedy action was of course essential to prevent the fire spreading to neighbouring roofs and every village had its fire hook for this emergency. Usually kept in the parish church, the hook was fixed to the end of a long pole and was used to remove the ignited covering from the roof. The main roof timbers were usually of oak and became charred rather than burnt, so it was a comparatively simple operation to repair the damage by replacing the supporting framework and thatch.

While thatch has been used in Devon since time immemorial, technical

An unusually large overhang has been added to the eaves of this cottage: an exaggerated feature popular with the Arts and Crafts Movement, but not often seen on an earlier building. Sampford Courtenay.

Details of the structural support to the thatched overhang above.

developments took place during the eighteenth century which led to the supply of alternative materials within the county. The quarrying of slate was a new industry and this, together with the revival of the process of baking clay (introduced by the Romans but long forgotten), undoubtedly had some effect on the thatching trade. As timber became easier to obtain for building purposes and less combustible materials became locally available, slate and tile began to replace thatch, which came to be regarded as inferior to these, particularly by the more affluent owners of large stone or brick houses. However, a complete reversal of this attitude occurred during the nineteenth century when the popularity of thatch was revived and it became a material of high fashion amongst the middle classes. This was largely a result of the publication of many 'house pattern books', which had a considerable influence on the population. These were the vehicle through which the Arts and Crafts Movement publicized the exaggerated rustic style of architecture known as 'cottage ornée', characterized by very steeply pitched, thatched roofs with enormous overhangs. The latter part of the nineteenth century continued with the return to the use of traditional materials and craftsmanship, in the style of building known as Art Nouveau, which followed a creed rejecting all the new technology of the Victorians.

Despite the changes brought about by building fashions and industrial developments, the limitations of cob and the remote locations of many stone

(Facing page) Cob and thatch ancillary farm building: the photograph dates from early this century. Iddesleigh.

Roadside shelter for milk churns with thatched roof and sides. Brampford Speke.

farmhouses have meant that the Devon thatcher has never been short of work. Until it gained widespread popularity, thatch was an inexpensive material and was used to roof all manner of structures. Ancillary farm buildings such as barns, granaries, pig and ash houses were all thatched; garden walls, too, often had a capping of thatch to protect them from the rain. Before the Dutch barn came into common use for storage purposes, even haystacks and thatch ricks had their own roofs of thatch. Since speed was of more importance here than quality of workmanship, farm labourers were often employed on this task and they made a cover similar to a mat which was fixed with plaited ropes of straw and twisted spars of hazel; the apex of the cover was completed with some form of ornamentation, usually in the shape of a bird or an animal, fashioned out of straw. Some thatchers today add a decorative straw 'dolly' to the ridge of a newly thatched roof, but this is more often done at the request of the owner, rather than being a traditional finishing touch. The master thatcher of former days tended to be more subtle with his trademark and provided nothing more elaborate than a hazel spar twisted into a simple shape and inserted at one end of the ridge.

Historically, a thatcher was always local to the area in which he worked and, as with cob building, the trade was often carried on by subsequent generations of the same family. Even today, there are many craftsmen in the trade who are following long family tradition, although the open-air life and the skills involved

Two ricks of wheat reed with thatched covers. Near South Molton.

are attracting many others with no such connection. The training requirements have changed hardly at all since the Middle Ages and a thatcher is not considered to be fully competent unless he has spent a period of time apprenticed to an experienced craftsman, followed by several years working to his direction; only after this rigorous training can a thatcher meet the high standards demanded by the Master Thatchers Association.

Garden wall with simple-style thatched capping and straw 'dolly'. Knowle.

Decorative thatched capping and straw 'dolly'. The apex of the thatch is covered with wire netting to protect it from potential damage by birds. Coleford.

Farmhouse at Newton Poppleford.

(*Facing page*) An unwanted
threshing machine.

4

THATCHING

As we saw in Chapter 3, the materials most commonly used for thatching today are long straw, water reed and combed wheat reed. Of these, long straw is the least enduring, lasting for only ten to twenty years, and for this reason may be considered to be uneconomic. Combed wheat reed is widely used in Devon and lasts from twenty-five to forty years, but the most superior thatch comes from a variety of water reed known botanically as *Phragmites communis* and this can provide a roof with a life of from fifty to sixty years.

As well as the type of material used, the life of the thatch depends on several other factors, including the pitch of the roof, the roof design, type and quality of material used, the local topography and the skill of the thatcher. Thatched roofs in the east of Britain will last longer than those in the west. The main reasons for this are that in the west there is higher than average rainfall, the topography means that many thatched houses are situated in deep valleys and are surrounded by trees with either a stream or a pond nearby, and roofs are of shallower pitch owing to the cob construction. Rot is the chief cause of deterioration in thatch, taking place only when high levels of moisture are present, so it can be seen that all these factors combine to shorten the life of thatch in the West Country.

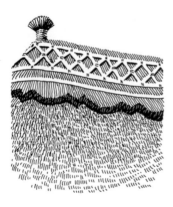

Phragmites communis grows naturally in coastal and riverside marshland, but for thatching purposes it has to be semi-cultivated. The reed grows 1–2½ metres tall and is harvested annually between January and March, after the frost has killed off the leaves and before the new shoots appear. Carried out on a regular basis, this operation prevents the beds from becoming clogged with dead reed and encourages the straight growth necessary for thatch.

Beds of pure *Phragmites communis* often contain two other varieties of related reed. These are reed mace (*Typha latifolia*) and wild iris (*Iris pseudocorus*). An admixture of these to the pure reed of up to 15 per cent is sometimes considered to be advantageous as far as both durability and appearance are concerned.

Water reed growing along the bank of the River Teign.

Thatching in progress: dressing
reed into position with a legget.
Sampford Courtenay.

Cottages at Newton St Cyres.

Threshing machine in operation
early this century. St Giles.

Until 1950, when the first mechanized cutting system was introduced, reed was traditionally harvested by hand by marshmen. The working conditions were difficult and unpleasant as the men had to stand knee deep in ice-cold water to cut the reed, but this method is still considered by some to produce the strongest thatch. However, since the late 1960s, when an amphibious harvester was introduced into this country from Denmark, the trade of marshman has largely given way to mechanization; more efficient than human labour, this machine is capable of cutting and binding between 2000 and 3000 bundles of reed per day.

There are many water-reed beds in Britain, although not all of them are large enough to yield appreciable quantities of thatching material. Reed beds in Dorset, Hampshire, Suffolk and parts of Wales are of sufficient size to keep the local thatchers supplied, but by far the largest and most well-known beds are in Norfolk. While some Devon roofs may be thatched with reed taken from small local beds, these are too insignificant in size to cater for the enormous demand in the county and most of the water reed used here is obtained either from Norfolk or from Europe. Until recently the environmental conditions of the East Anglian coast provided the thatcher with prime quality reed, but there is some concern that this may be adversely affected by the present-day use of agricultural fertilizers; these contain nitrates which seep into the water and reduce the life of the reed.

Combed wheat reed comes from an entirely different plant species from water reed and was originally a by-product of the wheat harvest. The traditional method of combing wheat by hand to remove the leaves and grain was laborious, but left the reed straight and unbroken; gathered and tied into bunches, it was then ready to be used for thatching. Present-day harvesting by combine is faster and more efficient as far as the collection of the grain is concerned, but it is useless for the provision of thatching material, as the stalks are left scattered in short lengths on the ground. The development of improved varieties of grain has also affected supplies of thatch; these tend to produce a better crop, but they have shorter and less pliable stalks which are unsuitable for thatch.

As a result of these modern agricultural processes, many Devon farmers set aside an area of land specifically for the cultivation of thatching reed, and while this is no longer tediously combed by hand, special methods of harvesting are employed to ensure that the reed is undamaged. With the attachment of a comber, an ordinary threshing machine can be used to remove the leaves and grain; this retains all the stalks with the butt ends laid in the same direction, ready to be tied together. Alternatively, a reaping and binding machine may be used; this does not thresh, but cuts and binds the wheat into bundles. When this has been done, the reed is stored on the farm for future use by the

Wheat reed for thatching, protected by its own thatched cover.

Cottages at Sidbury.

thatcher, usually in a Dutch barn, but occasionally in the traditional form of a rick, or stack, complete with its own thatched cover for protection from the weather.

There are similarities between the methods of application and the finished appearance of combed wheat reed and water reed thatch, but the bundles of each have different names and they are also measured in different units. A bundle of wheat reed is called a nitch, which weighs approximately 13 kg, whereas one of water reed is known as a bunch and is measured by its circumference – 600 mm in Britain, but 1 metre in Europe. To the layman these different units of measurement may be rather confusing, particularly as both cover areas of roof surface measured in square metres. However, in calculating the amount of thatch required, whether in bunches or nitches the

Bunches of water reed stored on site ready for use by the thatcher.

Reed mats and rolls used by the thatcher under the thatch and at the verge and ridge respectively.

end result is more or less the same, as the thickness or depth of the thatch is taken into account.

The process of thatching a roof is not one which can be rushed. The craftsmanship involved in using long-established techniques and natural materials takes time and care. Depending upon the size of the building and whether or not it has any special features such as dormer windows, the length of time needed will be anything from three weeks upwards. Weather conditions too must be taken into account and can understandably cause delays: rain or cold will cause the material to become respectively too damp or too stiff to handle, while windy conditions are difficult for the thatcher and make the thatch quite unmanageable.

The pitch of a thatched roof is always very steep so the rain and snow do not have a chance to settle and seep below the top surface. The ideal pitch for a thatched roof is between $50° - 60°$, but in the South West a pitch of about $45°$ is more usual. Moisture penetrates the thatch by capillary action; this should not be more than about 50 mm. It is important that thatch is not laid too tightly, for if it is compacted it does not have a chance to dry out or to breathe and thus allows a much deeper moisture penetration which reduces the life of the roof. The uneven surface means that rain-water does not flow down the roof, as it does on a smooth tile or slate cladding, but runs from reed to reed in a series of drops until it reaches the eaves. The wide overhang of the eaves ensures that the drops are thrown clear of the wall below and a gutter is rarely needed, except for the protection of passers-by where the roof overhangs a public footpath.

While the steep pitch may facilitate the shedding of snow and rain, it does not provide an easy working surface for the thatcher, who spends most of his time balanced on a slope of $45°$ or $50°$. The craft of thatching is particularly hard on the hands and knees and amongst his equipment the thatcher often has a special type of leather glove and knee pads for protection. Other materials and specialist tools are also very much part of the trade and different items are used for various stages of the work.

Before work on the roof commences, the butt ends of the bunches or nitches must be levelled and a 'spotboard' is used for this, the bundles of reed being tapped against the board in the same manner as a sheaf of paper is straightened. Water reed is ready for use after spotboarding, but wheat reed needs the additional preparation of being slightly dampened before it is placed on the roof. Rethatching work will also involve some preparation of the roof, to the extent of stripping off the old material down to a base of about 300 mm thick. The new thatch is fixed to the base with spars of split hazel or willow, which are similar in function to staples, pinning the new and old layers together.

The difference in colour between old and new thatch can be clearly seen in this cottage at Georgeham.

Woven reed mats used to face a cottage at Blackpool.

A selection of thatching tools, including (clockwise from top left): claw hammer – for driving iron spikes; twisted hazel spar; iron thatching hooks; leggett for dressing reed; shearing hook – for cleaning down face of finished work; thatcher's leather knee pad; shears; standing beadle.

The thatcher works from the eaves upwards towards the ridge of the roof, starting at the right-hand corner with a diagonally laid bundle of reed. As work proceeds up the slope of the roof, he will normally use a ladder or frame to lean on, which has spikes to anchor it into place on the thatch. The thatch itself must also be fixed: in new work, hazel or willow rods are placed horizontally across each course and either stitched through to the roof structure with treated cord or anchored with iron hooks. The fixing process involves the use of various types of specialist tools and the aid of an assistant, who is required to be within the roof space, particularly during stitching, to receive and return the needle and cord to the thatcher, working from the outside. A collection of needles of different lengths are needed for this operation. The reed is dressed into position throughout the laying process and for this a leggett is used: one type has a spiked surface for use with water reed and another type is grooved for combed wheat reed.

Fixing thatch to the rafters with an iron hook; the thatcher uses the standing beadle for support while working on the roof.

Dutch needle: used with tarred cord, this is a modern replacement for the traditional thatching needle and has the advantage that it can be operated by one person from the exterior of the roof.

Twisting a hazel spar into shape. Now obtained outside the county, hazel traditionally came from the many hedges which used to be a feature of the agricultural landscape.

Dressing water reed into position with a leggett. A combed wheat leggett has grooves instead of the studded surface shown here: many thatchers make their own water-reed leggetts, using personally preferred materials.

Cottage at Sampford Courtenay.

Cottage at Branscombe, showing the typical uneven surface of cob walls.

Rethatching in progress: a section of the lightweight supporting timbers is visible here. The three wooden frames which can be seen on the old thatch are 'standing beadles', which have two spikes to penetrate the thatch and are often used in place of a long ladder in the West Country.

Reed mats in position on the roof between the old and new thatch.

A new method imported from Holland and known as the 'Dutch needles method' is being used extensively today. One needle consists of a metal tube about 610 mm long and 20 mm in diameter, cut and shaped into a tapered needle. The other needle is a steel rod 10 mm in diameter by 610 mm long. The end of this rod is fashioned into a loop which is 45 mm in diameter. With a section of thatch loosely held in position the first needle is inserted above the batten, while the second is placed below. The two needles are then joined by placing the looped one over the other. Next a length of galvanized wire is pushed down by the first needle until it passes through the looped second needle. The first needle is now removed, leaving a good length of wire hanging over the thatch. The second needle is twisted and pulled out, bringing the wire with it. The two ends are then twisted together over the sway (a length of wood used to keep the line of thatch straight) and tightened down with a potato-bag twister. This method is very quick and dispenses with the need for an assistant inside the roof.

After the roof has been completed, the thatch is tidied up and trimmed with various types of hooks.

Thatcher laying bunches of water reed on an old roof. The fixing rods, hooks and spars can be seen here; also, in the top left-hand corner, the roll to the verge of the adjoining roof is just visible.

Thatching a new extension to an old thatched property. The roof timbers to the end of the roof are angled to produce a half-hip. The ridge roll can be seen already in position.

Thatching in progress: dressed reed on a roof.

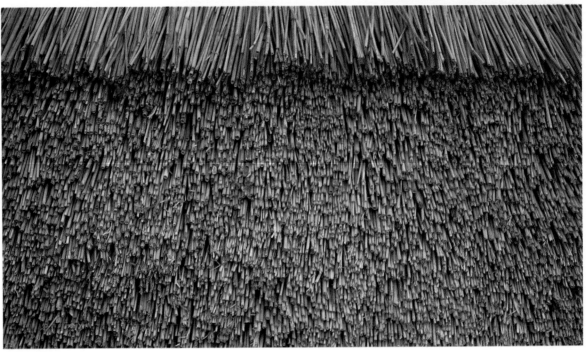

Rethatching a cottage at Harpford.

A thatching apprentice early this century. Note the protective knee pads he is wearing, similar to those worn today.

The ridge of the roof is often capped with a different type of thatch material from the main roof. The thatch is folded over the apex of the roof and thus needs to be easily pliable; threshed rye straw or sedge are suitable for this purpose, fixed into place with hazel or willow liggers on the outside surface. On some ridges the liggers may be fixed in a decorative pattern and other forms of ornament include the addition of a straw bird or animal, or the bottom edge of the capping might be cut into a pattern. The traditional Devon ridge, however, is plain, usually with several liggers simply running parallel with the roof. The ridge is the most vulnerable part of a thatched roof and will probably require some attention and repair long before the main pitches.

Thatched roofs in Devon can be hipped, gabled and, quite commonly, half-hipped, but generally speaking the older the roof structure the more likely it is to be hipped because of the early difficulties in forming a gable end. The eaves tend to be low, either immediately above the heads of the windows or even below, in which case the thatch is swept upwards in a curve over the window opening. Because it is hand crafted, in common with the cob walls that so often accompany it, it has the same informal and imprecise appearance and it weathers from a light to a medium golden-brown colour which blends with the rural landscape.

Thatcher applying a new ridge.

Examples of variations in dormer windows and ridges. The decorated ridge is not typical of Devon traditions, whereas the simpler style is, including the finials at the ends of the ridges. Harpford and Powderham.

Cottages at Broadclyst.

Cottage at Cockington.

5

MAINTENANCE, REPAIR AND RENOVATION

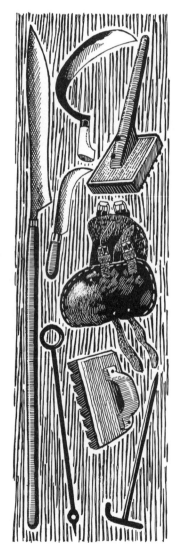

The previous chapters have outlined the history and the methods of building in cob and roofing with thatch. The practicalities of living in a house containing either or both of these materials will involve a higher degree of maintenance and repair than one of more recent date, although to those owners who enjoy living in a building with character, the additional benefits of warmth in winter, coolness in summer and natural insulation from noise, will probably outweigh any disadvantages as far as repair is concerned.

There are many vernacular cottages in Devon which have been 'modernized' at various times since they were built and it is still possible to find original features which have been concealed during this process, although these features will have been lost if the building has been gutted internally and the original layout altered. This type of drastic alteration is now regarded as near-vandalism and the result is often an over-prettified and unrealistic appearance. The aim of renovation and repair should be to carry out the work in the original manner, insofar as is possible, and to retain the basic character while returning the structure to good order. With this purpose in mind, it is always wise to obtain specialist advice and to employ skilled craftsmen with experience of working on old buildings; if their estimates seem expensive, this is likely to be not an inflated price but a realistic one because they will be aware of exactly what might be involved in any particular job. It should be remembered that the lowest price is not necessarily for the most thorough and efficient work and may be more costly in the long run, especially if the work proves to be unsatisfactory and has to be redone.

The vulnerability of cob if it becomes wet means that the combination of cob walls and thatched roof requires special vigilance to ensure that the thatch does

Two roofs in need of some attention: the eaves to the barn are beginning to disintegrate and could soon allow the penetration of damp to the top of the cob, while the central portion of the cottage roof needs repair, particularly below the chimney, where damp could penetrate to the roof-timbers.

Seventeenth-century timber
mullioned window in a cob wall;
the cob has been repaired with
stone.

not become damaged and allow water to penetrate to the cob or roof timbers. If after a long dry period subsequent rainfall causes a minor leak through an old portion of thatch, this will probably be a result of the compacted material having opened up and under these circumstances, need not necessarily be a matter for concern; more often than not, the fault will cure itself when the thatch becomes slightly damp again. On the other hand, especially if the house is in a heavily wooded area, a leaky patch might be traced to an actual hole in the thatch, which can be caused by birds seeking nesting material, and this will require professional repair. While awaiting the arrival of the thatcher, a temporary repair can be effected by filling the hole with a handful of straw and covering it with wire netting to prevent further attack on the looser material.

Treading cob at a demonstration at Mr A. Howard's premises, Morchard Bishop.

An overall roof covering of netting is sometimes seen, although this is not as common a practice in Devon as elsewhere in the country. This precaution against bird damage is less essential if the thatch is of water reed rather than combed wheat reed or long straw. Despite the higher incidence of attack by birds in wooded areas, thatchers usually advise against netting because of the danger of leaves and twigs becoming trapped and causing problems. Two points to bear in mind when deciding whether or not to net the thatch are that, besides the additional expense, it disguises to a certain extent the natural appearance and it may also hinder the flow of rain-water, which for the sake of the thatch should be as fast as possible, hence the steep pitch. However, it may be advantageous to wire the most vulnerable areas of the roof, such as the ridge and the surround to the chimney; the thatcher will be able to advise on this.

This roof is due for rethatching: the old thatch has deteriorated to such an extent that the fixing rods are visible.

Collapse of a thatched roof: some of the roof timbers have been affected, but it is interesting to note that while the portion of cob wall (above an opening in the stone below) has collapsed, the stone wall to the opposite side of the building is still intact. This cottage has since been rebuilt and renovated. Westleigh.

It is sensible to carry out routine inspections of the thatch about every five years, paying particular attention to the areas of greatest vulnerability. The ridge will in any event require replacing at approximately twelve-year intervals, but heavy storms can sometimes cause the ridge liggers to break and these must be replaced before they can penetrate the thatch and provide a course for rain-water to enter the roof space. Regular inspection will also reveal any other suspect areas and prompt attention to minor faults, even the simple expedient of removing any moss, may well have economic advantage in prolonging the life of the thatch.

Historically, thatch has always been considered to have a high risk of fire, but present-day statistics indicate no greater percentage of thatch fire than any other roof covering. However, thatch is more combustible and more often than not a fire can start from within the roof space rather than by ignition from outside. A defective chimney is sometimes responsible; this can allow heat to escape, which together with the superior insulating properties of thatch, can lead to an excessive increase of temperature to the point of combustion.

Removing old thatch from a roof early this century, possibly to replace it with another material: the importance of retaining thatch was not realized at that time. Landkey.

Woven reed mats have been utilized here to provide a temporary cover prior to rethatching. Georgeham.

Generally speaking, the older the house the more necessary it will be to inspect the state of the chimney regularly, particularly after a period of disuse. A chimney constructed in cob will be especially susceptible to extreme changes of temperature or humidity, and any cracks that appear in it are a potential source of danger; these of course should be repaired before the chimney is used again, either by pointing in mortar, or, if the damage is more fundamental, rebuilding in brick may be necessary.

As we saw earlier, when a roof is completely rethatched, the old material is stripped down to leave a base on which the new thatch is laid. There are, however, occasions when the thatcher may advise that the roof ought to be completely stripped and it is a good idea to take such an opportunity to lay a fire-resistant barrier between the roof timbers and the new thatch. Another advantage of stripping off the old material is that the state of the structural timbers can then be seen; these may not otherwise be accessible if, for instance, the roof space is sealed off from the rest of the house. Signs of defect may be shown by a sagging appearance in the thatch, although this does not always indicate faulty roof timbers, but may simply be due to the age of the roof or a result of settlement of the house over a period of time.

Should the structural roof timbers be found to have some damage, great care should be exercised in carrying out any repair. Because of the periodic renewal of thatch, it is impossible to date a building by this type of roof covering, nor is it easy to assess the age of cob walls, although in Devon a brick plinth rather than one of stone would indicate a building of a comparatively late date. The type of roof structure and the species of timber, however, can often provide important evidence towards estimating its age, and although this may not necessarily be conclusive as far as all the components of the house are concerned, it is usually a reliable method of establishing the origins of the building.

A cob barn in a state of deterioration: corrugated iron is often used to replace thatch on farm outbuildings and frequently covers old and disintegrated thatch.

The two chief causes of decay in timber are fungus and beetle. If the roof members show any signs of attack by either it is best to call in experts to identify the exact cause of the resultant rot and to recommend the correct treatment to eradicate the problem. It will not always be necessary to replace the affected member; in fact, in the case of a roof constructed before the eighteenth century, because of its probable historic interest, replacement should be carried out only as a very last resort.

Up to this period, a house built for one of the more affluent owners would often have been constructed with very substantial roof trusses or cruck frames and, provided that any areas of decay are not so extensive that the structural stability is weakened, the timbers are unlikely to be completely beyond repair. They may be found to have some form of decoration which would originally have been exposed to view, such as carving or painted motifs, while smoke blackening would indicate an early hall house of some importance; even the method of jointing may be unusual by today's standards and would therefore have historic importance. If any such features are discovered, the roof structure should be preserved if at all possible. The best method of repairing damaged areas is to remove each section of rotted timber, after ensuring that all trace of the fungus or beetle has been eradicated, and scarf in a new piece in the same variety of wood; an alternative type of repair may be carried out with the use of steel plating or strapping. A specialist carpenter who has experience of restoration work should be able to advise on the best technique and execute whatever repair is necessary.

Decay in roof timbers is not, of course, restricted to those sections within the roof space. The ends of rafters and the timber plate at the top of the wall to which the rafters are fixed, can be vulnerable to damp and subsequent rot if the thatch at the eaves is allowed to deteriorate; this in turn can lead to major defects to cob, particularly if the condition is allowed to continue for any length of time. The need to provide a large overhang to thatched eaves, so that rainwater is directed away from the walls below, was mentioned earlier; it follows, therefore, that any damage which occurs at the eaves will reduce the amount of protection to the walls. Furthermore, there is the possibility that gradual disintegration of the damaged area of thatch will follow, and should this happen, the damp will penetrate the top of the wall and cause cob to lose its stability.

While it is usual to carry out most building repair work in matching material, because of the shrinkage which occurs when new cob dries out alternatives have to be used for rebuilding damaged cob walls. The one exception to this is any replacement at the top of the wall, for which cob can be used, because the procedure of building up a layer in new cob is basically the same as the original method used to construct the wall. However, even if the location of the damage requires other materials to be used, it is important to remember that the

The upper portion of this barn has been rebuilt in cob. Sigford.

proper repair of cob requires knowledge and understanding of its characteristics, and it should not be attempted by a builder who is used only to working with modern pre-formed materials.

Damp penetration is probably the most common cause of cob failure and it also causes damage to the exterior plaster finish. Any cracking, bulging or signs of decay in the plaster may be indicative of dampness behind it, which will erode the cob after a time. Conversely, it might mean that the fault lies with the cob, possibly the result of earlier work, such as an incorrect or hastily executed repair. Defective material must always be removed and taken down to a sound base before it is replaced, otherwise before long there will be a recurrence of the same problem.

On occasions, where the cob has been in a state of neglect for any length of time, the complete collapse of a section of wall may ensue. Rebuilding can be carried out in brick, stone or concrete block, and while the latter may seem at odds with the basic nature of cob, its advantage is that it is light in weight, so it will not add too much loading on the cob on which it is built up. Concrete in any other form, however, such as pre-cast lintols or window cills, should not be used in conjunction with cob. Structural movement in cob usually results from

A corner of a farm outbuilding before and after renovation and rethatching. Gittisham.

some change in the stability of either the subsoil or the roof structure and can often be halted by the addition of a buttress to support the wall.

At the opposite end of the scale of repair, minor cracks in cob are fairly simple to deal with by infilling with a weak mortar mix. In the case of wider cracks, one of the best methods of joining the separated edges is to form a link with courses of roofing tiles bedded in mortar. Shallow erosions on the face of the wall may either be accepted as being characteristic of the irregularities of cob, or can be made good with a lime mortar mix. Points worth noting in connection with any repair of cob are that after having removed all unsound material, work should be commenced only on a clean and dampened surface; also, care should be taken to reproduce the uneven appearance of the old cob – a plumb and smooth face will result in the area of repair looking obvious. The finished appearance of the exterior plaster is equally important: it should never have a pattern, such as is sometimes seen. A wood float, instead of a modern steel trowel, should be used to achieve the traditional flat finish.

Damp penetration is caused not only by leaking roofs, cracks or faulty plaster, but can also occur through the base of the wall. If there is evidence of damp at this point, the cause may be traced to a leaking water pipe below ground level or, more simply, to a build up of earth above the plinth and might, for instance, be the result of a flower bed having replaced the traditional cobbled drainage strip around the perimeter of the house walls. Modern building technology is not usually suited to cob and it is inadvisable to install a damp-proof course because this can lead to the walls becoming too dry. If the trouble persists after clearance of any obstruction above the plinth, specialist advice should be obtained.

In an early cottage, the ground floor may be subject to rising damp. There can be many reasons for this: the floor may be laid directly on earth and it may be affected because of rising damp in the walls, or the dampness may originate from some outside source quite unconnected with any fault in the house itself, such as a recent diversion of underground water courses, perhaps resulting from nearby building operations. The insertion of a damp-proof membrane here might serve only to transmit the damp back to the walls, so again it is best to get a professional opinion on both the cause and the remedy.

As mentioned earlier, roof timbers can provide information which is helpful in dating the origins of a house or cottage, and this is also true of certain interior features. Some early houses which have a three-room and cross-passage plan, may contain the original timber partitions, sometimes found concealed behind later laths and plaster. Known as plank and muntin screens, they may have been affected by any rising damp through the floor and the cill and base of the screen members may be decayed. As with roof timbers, any early timber screens should be preserved; after the removal of the affected areas, they can

A lime plaster should be used on cob, otherwise the result will be as illustrated here.

A timber plank and muntin screen: the horizontal marking indicates that the screen has been covered with lath and plaster. Newton St Cyres.

A wall painting discovered in a sixteenth-century house when damp caused many subsequent coatings to disintegrate. Branscombe.

A moulded plaster ceiling dating from the seventeenth century. Christow.

be repaired by carefully splicing in new matching timber sections. In order to prevent any possibility of the new cill suffering damage from damp, a strip of proofing membrane can be inserted below it without adversely affecting any other part of the building.

Plank and muntin screens sometimes have quite simple detail, but occasionally more complicated mouldings or painted decoration are incorporated, indicating that the original owner of the house was probably quite wealthy. Painted decoration on an interior plaster surface has the same significance. Often all trace of painting will have disappeared from view over the centuries, only to come to light again when the plaster or timber is being cleaned. Naturally such decoration has great historic value and if any is found, both further cleaning and restoration should be left to an expert, who will be able to renovate the designs using the original muted colours.

The renovation and repair of a cob and thatch house or cottage can be both satisfying and rewarding, particularly if some unsuspected feature is discovered, but it is as well to understand that, owing to the age of the building and the nature of the materials, repairs may lead to more work than is at first foreseen. In certain circumstances, even this factor may be turned to advantage. If, for instance, additional accommodation is being considered, it may be opportune to extend rather than rebuild or repair a suspect wall. The rather sensitive subject of extension is dealt with in the following chapter.

6

ALTERATIONS AND EXTENSIONS

We have seen that the existence of particular features in cob and thatch houses may provide clues to the date of the original building. Equally, of course, certain items and specific methods of construction may be discovered which are not consistent with the date of other parts of the structure. These will probably indicate that the building has been altered during its life and they can also give some idea of when this occurred.

The first home improvements were carried out during the late fifteenth century to a form of structure which, for about 500 years, had provided nothing more than very basic shelter. In Devon alterations to enhance living conditions were prompted by an improvement in the financial standing of the sheep

This large farmhouse appears to have been built as one structure, but whereas the core probably dates from the sixteenth century, major alteration took place during the mid and late seventeenth and early eighteenth centuries. Listed Grade II*, the listing includes the cob garden wall to the left. Pyne Farmhouse, Washford Pyne.

farmer, who had little else but his home on which to spend his new-found wealth. Later, other influences came along and amongst those of subsequent centuries were the varying dictates of fashion in building styles, developments in methods of transportation, advances in building technology and, not least, the more recent effects of building regulations. However, most of these factors became far more evident in town architecture and only marginally affected the cob houses in rural areas; the latter developed at a much slower rate, some influences taking as long as 100 years to reach the most remotely situated cottages.

Present-day trends have had a much greater effect. Even the most rurally located houses lie within easy reach of a town, and commuting is now an accepted way of life, so the erstwhile usually unattainable dream of owning a thatched country cottage has become a definite possibility for many people. This change in circumstances sometimes has very real drawbacks as far as the cottage itself is concerned; it is rarely suited in all respects to the requirements of its new owner, so he probably sets about making alterations, sometimes

Built as one house in the seventeenth century or possibly earlier, the original three-room, cross-passage plan has been extended at each end and a two-storey porch added, probably at the location of the cross-passage. Early this century, the shop display window was installed in the porch. The house is now divided into two dwellings. Listed Grade II. Oakdene, Broadclyst.

with disastrous results for the character of the cottage which attracted him in the first place. For instance, the cottage may not be quite large enough without the addition of a room or two, but if it is not suitably designed, an extension – however small – can seriously upset the scale of the building. The choice of materials is another area where mistakes can be made and the replacement of traditional materials with cheaper modern versions can completely alter the character of the cottage. Equally damaging in this respect, are lavish and extravagant details which serve only to provide an over-decorated and unrealistic appearance.

No set patterns can be followed when making alterations to old buildings. The reason for this is that, in direct contrast to today's housing, most cottages of pre-Victorian era were constructed by local craftsmen in an individual manner, therefore each has to be assessed on its individual merits: what is a suitable style of alteration for one may be completely unsympathetic for another.

The environs of the building also need to be taken into account: there may be features of the site on which it stands which make it more difficult to extend in one direction than another. In addition there may be constraints on the design of any proposed alterations and extensions. The preservation of the character of its traditional buildings is important to Devon's heritage, and with this aim in mind, many have been Listed by the Department of the Environment on the basis of their historic or architectural interest. Of course, not all cob and thatch cottages have retained enough of their original intrinsic value to be listed, but some may be considered to contribute to the general character of a Conservation Area, which will have been designated to preserve the appearance of a village or town. Contrary to what is generally believed, alterations are usually allowed to buildings falling into Listed and/or Conservation categories, but extra vigilance is exercised at the planning application stage to ensure that what is proposed will not result in any damaging effects similar to those mentioned earlier.

So, apart from their obvious historical interest, what exactly is the quality of these cob and thatch houses which warrants their preservation and a sensitive approach to their alteration? Much of their character is more easily illustrated than described, but undoubtedly part of their attraction is that they seem to belong to the Devon landscape; long, low and undulating, they fit into the topography and this is where one of the major problems of extension makes itself apparent. New building works today are subject to requirements laid down in the Building Regulations and those regulations concerning the height of habitable rooms provide one of the greatest difficulties in making an extension appear to belong to the original building and not seem to be over-assertive. Many old cottages have ceiling heights which are less than the minimum

A group of basically sixteenth-century cottages with later alterations: variations in the shape and form of the roof could only be achieved in thatch. The sweep from ridge to ground floor is a typical method of roofing a lean-to type of extension and is known as a catslide. Listed Grade II. The Square, Drewsteignton.

allowed today, so that unless the new ground floor can be set below that of the old, a two-storey extension will result in the addition being higher overall than the original. A more sensitive way of dealing with this particular problem is to limit the addition to one storey only. If, however, alteration or renovation involving room heights is intended within an old building – say, in the event that the first-floor construction has collapsed – then it is possible to obtain a wayleave, which will allow the replacement of the floor at its original level, even though this may result in a lower than usual room height above and below.

Of course there are many ways of extending a house or cottage and how this can be achieved will depend not only upon the layout of the building and the available space around it, but also upon the amount and type of extra accommodation which is required, the style of the building and that of the extension, the most suitable materials to use, and so on. Such a project is often fraught with difficulties unforeseen by an amateur – albeit an enthusiastic one – and just as expert advice should be sought for repairs, it is also advisable to consult an architect about alterations, preferably one who has both experience of this type of work and a genuine feeling for old buildings.

The overall size as well as the height of an extension is critical in its relationship to the original building; it should never dominate and will be most successful if it is of subsidiary proportions, provided, of course, that the detailing is in character. Looking at the outside of any cob house which, at first glance, seems not to have been altered at all, it is often difficult to detect an area of extension, particularly if some time has elapsed since the work was done. This is partly due to the natural weathering process which has resulted in the later components blending with the older portion, but it also has a lot to do with traditional craftsmanship and the use of natural rather than manufactured materials. Houses and cottages have been extended in a variety of ways in past centuries, from the functional single-storey outshot to the later fashion-influenced additions such as a large porch, and from the simple addition in matching style of an extra bay on the end of a cottage to the considerable enlargement of a house by the addition of a wing or two. The latter was an expensive operation carried out only by wealthy owners of houses which were comparatively large in the first place, and was usually accompanied by a complete refurbishment of the original building. The former, however, are more modest methods of enlargement and are quite commonly seen.

Before the mass production of artificial materials began, regional variations in the appearance of buildings was confined to render, stone, brick, slate and timber, but the range of building components available today presents what can be a very confusing choice, particularly if they are viewed amongst a profusion of small samples at a builders' merchants. Whether extending or making alterations, it is both easiest and wisest to select exterior finishes, as well as patterns of doors and windows, which are either consistent or compatible with the original build. Thus new exterior walls may be constructed of concrete block but the finish applied to the outside face should be a render similar to that of the cob walls. If the cottage already features some brick or stone, then this might be repeated in any new work, but with caution and only in small quantities; second-hand or stock bricks will provide the best match for old weathered brickwork, while care must be taken to lay natural stone in the traditional manner – nothing looks worse than a stone wall having the appearance of vertical crazy paving with masses of mortar visible on the surface.

New windows should have timber frames; plastic or aluminium will not accommodate any movement in cob walls satisfactorily, nor will they appear compatible with existing windows if used for an extension. In size, proportion and emphasis – horizontal or vertical– they should respect existing windows and be limited in number to avoid dominating areas of solid wall; only in cases

Some minor extensions in character with the main building, with thatched or slate roofs. East Anstey, Sheepwash, Ottery St Mary and Tipton St John.

where a large opening exists – as might be found in a barn which is being converted – should large areas of glazing be contemplated as an infill, set well back from the face of the wall. Best avoided altogether are those standard ranges which masquerade under names such as 'Georgian'; these are divided into small panes of proportions which bear no relationship to those of genuine Georgian panes and will contrast oddly if used alongside the real thing. Similarly, those styles of standard front doors claiming to resemble traditional patterns do not suit cottages of basically simple character.

Sometimes a building to which alterations are proposed may already have had changes made to it in the past. In such a case, if different materials or

This cottage has been extended in the same style as the original. The new area of thatch is lighter in colour, but this will darken with the effects of weathering. Listed Grade II. Perrymans One, Georgeham.

window types have been introduced, it is difficult to decide which period of building should influence further works. Generally speaking, if these seem compatible, simple details which reflect certain aspects of both will work best, but the rule of assessing each case on its individual merits still applies. If the later alterations seem to be completely out of character, the course of action which will provide the most satisfactory end result will be the removal of the most offending features as part of the proposed new work. This may sound rather daunting in terms of cost, but an experienced architect may be able to suggest a comparatively easy and economical solution, which will be less irritating to live with and therefore cost effective in the long run.

As far as roof finishes are concerned a temptation to replace existing thatch should be resisted. Any other material will introduce a rigid appearance at odds with the unevenness of cob walls, while some alternatives which are heavier

A previous use of this long range of eighteenth-century outbuildings was as a malthouse: it has been recently converted to housing units, with some new door and window openings being inserted alongside those already existing, thus providing a pleasant, slightly haphazard appearance. Listed Grade II. The Maltings, Crediton.

could ultimately be more costly. These might involve either replacement or at least strengthening of the existing roof timbers, which in time might prove to add too much extra loading for the cob walls to carry, resulting in serious problems of collapse. Should the house or cottage be Listed, the removal of thatch will certainly be discouraged, but it is possible that some financial assistance in the form of a grant towards the cost of rethatching may be available from the local District Council.

Unless it is particularly desirable, and suited to the building, the roof to an extension need not necessarily be thatched. Where an extra bay is added and the roof is lengthened at the same height, it will be both practical and aesthetically pleasing to continue the thatch to the new bay, but otherwise natural slate – used in the past to roof outshots and porches to thatched buildings – will blend well. Artificial slates, although now improving, tend to relate unsympathetically to cob cottages, owing to their over-large size and slightly shiny appearance. Definitely to be avoided are large concrete tiles, which are far too dominant, producing an alien scale and jarring element, particularly those which are moulded in a pattern.

Finally, when undertaking works of alteration or extension, it is as well to be prepared for delays in the anticipated length of contract. The disturbance of any part of a structure which has been in existence for a considerable length of time – even an apparently simple operation such as the provision of a new door opening – means that it is always possible that some historical feature may be uncovered; this will not only cause some excitement, but may also necessitate some alteration to the original proposals.

7

RECENT DEVELOPMENTS

The earlier chapters of this book have outlined the traditions of building with cob and roofing with thatch, traditions which were adhered to for many centuries, until the new technology which developed during the Victorian era became responsible for the introduction of various changes. This was the beginning of a pattern which has continued ever since and at an ever-increasing rate. This being the case, can there be a place for such traditional building materials in the future?

If current trends are anything to go by, the considerable interest in both conservation and the ingeniousness of all traditional crafts seems to indicate that many will survive. Thatching is almost certainly a trade which will always be in demand, provided of course that the supply of material is guaranteed. The future of cob, however, is a different matter and it seems doubtful that it will ever regain popularity as a constructional material in this country in more than a very minor way, chiefly because of the time element involved. After all, the appearance of rendered cob, particularly that which has been constructed with the aid of shuttering, can be very similar to any other like-coated material, whereas thatch is visually unique. Also, in spite of the periodic attention afforded to cob since its general demise during the nineteenth century, none of these brief resurgencies of interest in it has been at all influential in prompting a substantial revival of cob building. This is undoubtedly due to the difficulties caused by the combination of the lengthy drying-out process and the often inclement weather, which obviously compares unfavourably with the speed with which houses can be built by other methods. In the present era of large-scale housing developments, time and finance are one and the same and the use of cob would be quite impractical on an economic basis, except perhaps as an exclusive and highly priced sales gimmick. In the category of minor structures,

Members of the former Architect's Department of Devon County Council laying unbaked clay bricks at the experimental site at Bicton College of Agriculture.

however, the traditional method of building with cob is being maintained and the skills and knowledge of local craftsmen are made available to interested members of the public through the Devon Rural Skills Trust, which arranges occasional demonstration days of thatching, cob and other building and agricultural traditions.

This is not to say that experimentation with a view to improving methods of earth building has ceased. On the contrary, there has been recent activity in this field at an international level, with particular reference to those countries south of the equator that have long traditions of mud building, and the problems that currently affect them. Here in this country cob projects have been carried out under community programmes using local labour; an experiment which was perhaps reminiscent of Clough Williams-Ellis's theory on the usefulness of unbaked earth in times of shortage was undertaken in 1976 by the Architect's Department of Devon County Council.

This experiment set out to investigate the structural and thermal qualities of a specially constructed building of unfired clay, while simultaneously carrying out an energy-saving exercise. It was perhaps proof of the basic disadvantages involved with using cob in the traditional manner that the decision was taken to use standard clay bricks, unbaked but dried in the exhaust from the kilns in order to accelerate the drying process. The project building was sited within the grounds of Bicton College of Agriculture, where it is now in use as a store. Two years after completion the conclusions drawn from the experiment were that while the use of unfired clay constituted a saving in energy – although in this instance the saving was partly theoretical, since it made use of an energy-consuming operation – the use of stablized earth blocks, containing a percentage of cement, would probably be more successful and cause fewer problems in several respects during construction.

Unlike cob, thatch has been in continual use for many centuries and has not attracted much attention or experimentation until fairly recently. The effects of modern harvesting methods on wheat reed, and the use of fertilizers in the area of the Norfolk water-reed beds, have already been mentioned; the possibility that these factors may cause a future shortage of suitable reed for thatching purposes has partly prompted the research currently in progress. At the University of Bath microbiologists are carrying out a three-year programme of investigation into the effects of both nitrogenous fertilizers and varying climatic conditions on thatching materials. It has already been established that the addition of nitrogen, which increases the growth of the strain of wheat seed currently used, allows water to penetrate a thatched roof to a depth of 125–150 mm instead of the acceptable 25 mm. An experiment on Butser Hill in East Hampshire, has been concentrated on the revival of Medieval methods of cultivating and harvesting wheat and included a project of building and thatching a circular stone shelter. This structure is very similar to a farm building on Braunton Great Field, a site in North Devon of archaeological interest. Here the stone walling was all that remained, until a recent community programme provided labour which, under the direction of a master thatcher, constructed new roof timbers and a thatched roof.

Cottages of cob and thatch, stone and thatch, and – of later date – brick and thatch, provide the image of Devon's traditional buildings, but new houses with thatched roofs are seen infrequently. There are many reasons for this, a major one being the requirements as far as modern building regulations are concerned. In this respect, the potential hazard of fire has until recently been difficult to overcome, but this can now be combated by the provision of heavy-gauge aluminium foil, which is fixed to the battens below the thatch. This method of meeting fire regulations has been used in a small executive-type housing development at Milton Keynes, recently built by a nationally known

Circular stone linhay, dating from
the early nineteenth century,
recently rethatched by Community
Programme labour. Listed Grade II.
Braunton Marsh.

firm. It is interesting to note also that the Norfolk-reed thatch was treated with a chemical to deter moss, mould and lichen growth. It must be stressed, however, that the incorporation of a fire barrier is not always possible when rethatching an old roof, nor is the chemical treatment of reed always advisable, and it is best to take the advice of the thatcher on the suitability of these items.

At present some Devon farmers are growing wheat reed specifically for local thatching purposes, but there still remains a national shortage in the provision of ancillary services and materials within the trade. Several farmers in the county have recognized the need for threshing and combing services and they maintain their own machines, chiefly to process their own reed, but occasionally also undertaking this work on a contractual basis outside the county in areas where this facility is not available.

Currently, the nationally cultivated supply of water reed is being supplemented by the importation of Continental reed, but supplies of hazel – the best material for the spars, liggers and sways which are used to fix the thatch in position – are very scarce. The tradition of hazel coppicing, which provided a supple wood for many other purposes besides those connected with thatching, has almost disappeared, and it is only recently that the cultivation of hazel has recommenced in some parts of the country, but so far this is on too small a scale to meet demands. The alternative materials which are being utilized at present are willow, which is sufficiently pliable to be twisted into

A recently constructed thatched house which successfully reflects traditional scale and proportions. The windows used here are from a standard range which is particularly suited to buildings in sensitive areas, although a deeper window reveal is more characteristic. Gittisham.

These two photographs illustrate quite clearly the importance of adopting a sensitive approach to renovation work. The cottage below was originally similar in character to those in the terrace above, but it has lost its identity in the plastic thatch roof, the unsympathetic type of window, the rigid concrete tiles to the lean-to roof, the mock period door and the metal garage door. The terrace of cottages shows some variation from the original detailing, but this is unobtrusive and in character. A natural thatched roof, similar to that over the door, is currently available as a prefabricated item, but as it is of a standard design, this may not reflect local traditions. Top — Dolton; bottom — near Witheridge.

spars, and iron reinforcement rods, which are used as sways for binding the courses of thatch. The latter are concealed by each subsequently laid course and so they are neither visible nor exposed to damp, but as there is nothing to equal hazel in terms of quality and durability, there seems to be an opportunity to fill a gap in the market here and recommence hazel coppicing as a viable trade.

It is probably worth mentioning – if only to discourage its use – a comparatively recent product called plastic thatch, introduced some twelve or so years ago when there was a shortage of master thatchers. Whereas it did not have the potential disadvantages of natural thatch, equally it had none of the attractions either. It was not, as its name might suggest, a system of thatching with separate reeds of plastic (that has been investigated and as yet not found to be satisfactory); this was a form of sheet roofing, moulded on the top surface to give the appearance of reed. As is the case with many plastics used outdoors, the effects of weathering by sun and rain caused some loss of colour and a tendency for the surface to look shiny and slightly transparent, which characteristics had little enough in common with the real thing, but the difference between the two materials was really emphasized by a hardness of line and shadow never seen on a roof of natural thatch. Thankfully this alternative did not achieve much popularity in Devon and a mere glance at the illustration of one of the few examples in the county will probably suffice as an explanation.

During the past few years, public awareness of the importance of conserving all aspects of building traditions has resulted in a much more sensitive range of products becoming available. Traditional designs in natural materials can now be obtained from firms specializing in a variety of items for both interior and exterior renovation works, from decorative plasterwork to ironmongery and from chimney pots to garden gates. In addition, there is a lively market in architectural salvage and there are firms all over the country specializing in the reclamation of building materials, fixtures and fittings for resale. With the wide choice currently available, it should usually be possible to find a suitable design of whatever item is required, either new or reclaimed, to conserve the basic character of the building which is undergoing renovation.

Lastly, but by no means of the least consideration to owners of thatched properties, some insurance companies have developed a more realistic attitude towards thatch; the previously held view that thatch is more frequently affected by fire damage than other roofing materials is no longer so prevalent. Provided that normal safety requirements are satisfied, it is possible to obtain more favourable rates from those firms which offer specialist insurance.

BIBLIOGRAPHY

Devon's Heritage (Devon County Council, 1982)

Devon's Traditional Buildings (Devon Books, 1988)

The Thatcher's Craft (Cosira, 1960)

Bowyer, Jack *Vernacular Building Construction* (Architectural Press, 1980)

Clifton-Taylor, Alec *The Pattern of English Building* (Faber, 1972)

Cunnington, Pamela *Care for Old Houses* (Prism Alpha, 1984)

Cunnington, Pamela *How Old Is Your House?* (Alphabooks, 1980)

McCann, John *Clay and Cob Buildings* (Shire Publications, 1983)

Williams-Ellis, E. & Field, Eastwick *Building in Cob, Pisé and Stabilised Earth* (1919)

INDEX

Page numbers in italic refer to photographs.